IMAGES OF King's Lynn

Eastern Daily Press

IMAGES OF

King's Lynn

The Breedon Books
Publishing Company
Derby

First published in Great Britain by
The Breedon Books Publishing Company Limited
Breedon House, 44 Friar Gate, Derby, DE1 1DA.
1996

ISBN 1 85983 052 8

Printed and bound by Butler & Tanner Ltd., Selwood Printing
Works, Caxton Road, Frome, Somerset.

Colour separations by Colour Services, Wigston, Leicester.

Jackets printed by Lawrence-Allen, Weston-super-Mare, Avon.

Contents

Dedication

To Pat Midgley and John Smallwood,
for their inspirational love of the past.

Acknowledgements

I would like to thank the Eastern Counties Newspapers photographic department for their ever-efficient service when dealing with photographs for this volume, and special thanks to chief photographic technician Diane Townsend. John Hocknell and Tony Kemp have given generously of their time in helping my research, and Steve Addison, Carol Day and John Grimes have helped with specific queries. Sylvia Roberts kindly helped check the manuscript. And of course, to my wife Velma, who has tolerated occasionally severe disruption to her household routine.

Photographs

Any of the photographs used in this book can be purchased from the photographic department, Eastern Counties Newspapers, Prospect House, Rouen Road, Norwich NR1 1RE.

Introduction

IN THE 1960s the then King's Lynn Town Council brought out a guidebook to the borough, taking the theme *The many faces of Lynn*. It was an apt choice, as that is exactly what Lynn has. Even the name shows it – King's Lynn is the formal name, but to generations of ordinary Linnets it is simply 'Lynn'.

That 1960s guide picked out the following: The historical face, the visiting face, the holiday face, the shopping face, the seafaring face and the industrial face. Lynn is all these, and more.

The *Eastern Daily Press*, Norfolk's own daily newspaper, has recorded these aspects of the town's life over generations, and this book brings you around 300 of the most evocative *EDP* pictures from the 1950s, 1960s and 1970s, with some from the 1940s too.

Every reader will know from his or her experiences just how turbulent these decades have been. Old ways of life have crumbled, until sometimes it seems the only certainty in life is its uncertainty. Lynn has proved no exception to the rule.

For centuries the town used its position at the head of the extensive Great Ouse river basin to ensure a measure of prosperity, although nothing approached its halcyon days in the medieval period when it was one of the leading ports in England.

The upheavals of the twentieth century – and the effect of two world wars and boom-and-bust economic cycles – forced a change of heart. From the 1950s Lynn tried with renewed vigour to woo new employers and investment to the town. The first major success was the arrival of Campbell's Soups in 1959. Dow Chemical soon followed, along with a plethora of other firms.

A 'London overspill' agreement brought a sharp increase in the population of the town, although not to some of the levels predicted at one stage. Land prices soared, new housing and industrial estates sprang up around the outskirts of the town.

Of course, the 1960s expansion had its price. For example, fine old buildings were swept away in the drive to 'move with the times'. But the supporters of the change argue that Lynn had to expand – or suffer the fate of being a slowly-declining rural backwater.

Whatever the pros and cons of the changes, it is fortunate that the *EDP* has been there to record them for posterity.

The Lynn office of the paper has been blessed with many fine photographers over the period, notably Claude Fisher, Tony Kemp, Alan Howard, John Hocknell and Brian Waite, and this book includes a cross-section of their work taken over more than 40 years.

Each has brought his own individual and distinctive approach to the task of recording the big – and small – events in Lynn's life. There are important photographs in this volume recording the last days of now-lost Lynn streets. And days of drama, too, such as the 1953 floods. But *Images of King's Lynn* aims also to bring many pictures detailing the lives of ordinary Lynn folk, from the cheering crowds of a school sports day to the smiling regulars of a town centre pub.

Despite all the changes, it is also reassuring just how many things about Lynn life have stayed much the same over the years. The Mart delights every February, King's Lynn Football Club still gives its supporters plenty of ups and downs, the ancient markets provide a twice-weekly heartbeat to the shopping life of the town, and the fishing fleet still harvests the riches of the sea as it has done for centuries.

You will meet many well-known faces in these pages; some famous ones too. And, of course, there will be hundreds of faces and places in these pages with a special and personal meaning for readers.

It's Lynn's story. But it's your story too.

Trevor Heaton
Summer 1996

Royal Lynn

IT WAS back in the reign of Henry VIII that the old Bishop's Lynn became King's Lynn, but the royal links go back centuries before that. And those royal ties are just as strong today. Since the last century the position of Lynn so close to Sandringham has ensured a royal presence few comparable towns can match. This has manifested itself in a large number of formal events – such as the 1954 Freedom ceremony which begins our selection – but the town has also enjoyed a plethora of informal visits, whether the sight of young royal children arriving at Lynn railway station for their Christmas and New Year holiday, or the Queen Mother visiting her beloved Lynn Festival.

If there is one member of the Royal Family who has been more closely associated with Lynn than any other, then it must be without question the Queen Mother. She has made literally dozens of trips to the town, but one of the most special was on 26 July 1954 when the Borough of King's Lynn, which was celebrating the 750th anniversary of its first charter, admitted her to the status of Honorary Freeman – the first time the title had been bestowed on a woman. Our picture shows the Queen Mother with mayor Mr B.E.Bremner waving at the crowds from the steps of the Corn Exchange.

The royal car makes its way across the Tuesday Market Place to the cheers of hundreds of onlookers. After receiving her honour, the Queen Mother said: "King's Lynn, which lies so close to the home where I have spent many, many happy days, holds a special place in my heart."

Another chapter in an historic day: The Queen Mother and Princess Margaret listen to Ruth, Lady Fermoy shortly after the Queen Mother had unveiled the portrait of Lady Fermoy, painted by Anthony Devas. The Queen Mother paid tribute to Lady Fermoy's vision and hard work in rescuing the Guildhall of St George from oblivion Lady Fermoy was Princess Diana's grandmother and a friend and lady-in-waiting to the Queen Mother.

Ruth, Lady Fermoy, accompanies the Queen Mother to an event in the Guildhall of St George in January 1956. The Guildhall is the centre for many of the events in the annual King's Lynn Festival, held every July, and which Lady Fermoy helped establish as a superb arts event which regularly attracts world-renowned artists.

The Duke of
Edinburgh greets the
crowds on arrival at
the Guildhall of St
George in a picture
taken around 1960.

Lynn had one of the first
glimpses of royal husband-to-
be Anthony Armstrong-Jones
in early January 1962 when he
joined his new fiancée
Princess Margaret for the royal
New Year Holiday.

Royal-to-be: The 27-year-old Katharine Worsley – with Princess Alexandra – arrives at Lynn station on 1 January 1961, a few months before her marriage to the Duke of Kent.

For years the arrival of the Royal Family at Lynn station for their annual Christmas and New Year holiday at Sandringham provided a tailor-made chance for the public to see them at close range. On 30 December 1966, the royal party arrived to be met by the Lord Lieutenant of Norfolk, Sir Edmund Bacon – and an expectant crowd hoping for some fine pictures. The Queen holds the hand of a young Prince Edward, clearly fascinated by the train.

Princess Margaret takes care of Lady Sarah Armstrong-Jones.

Top: A hint of hoped-for Yuletide pleasures with the loading of a sledge among the royal luggage. Bottom: Crowds await the Royals.

The Queen Mother braved showers to pay an informal visit to Lynn Festival on 30 July 1966. She listened to a recital by St Margaret's Church organist Brian Hesford and toured a calligraphy exhibition at the Guildhall of St George. After admiring the beautiful writing on display, she was asked to sign the visitors' book. "I don't know if I dare!" she quipped.

Long may she reign: Even the January raindrops cannot hide the familiar beaming smile of the Queen in this unusual study taken as she left Lynn railway station in January 1972.

Prince Edward had gained in height – and self-assurance – when he arrived at the station on 20 January 1970 ready for the royal train's return to London.

Musical milestone: The Queen Mother chats to Ruth, Lady Fermoy and oboist Evelyn Rothwell after Lady Fermoy – a fine concert pianist – and the oboist had put on the 25th anniversary lunchtime concert at the Guildhall of St George in January 1971.

The Duchess of Kent insisted on informality when she agreed to open the WI Norfolk Federation's Lynn area exhibition in October 1973 – and this photograph showed she did just that. The Duchess, who had just joined the movement, is shown talking to Mrs H.Towler, chairman of the handicraft part of the exhibition. The two-day display took place in Lynn Town Hall.

The Duke of Edinburgh shares a joke with a worker on an Anglia Canners production line during his visit on 3 November 1978. The Duke was visiting the factory, and Anglia Frozen Foods, to see how the pea crop from the Royal Estate was processed. His packed five and a half hour schedule also included a visit to Campbell's Soups.

How do they do that? Fascination on the face of Princess Margaret as she watches hand-moulding in progress during her tour of the Wedgwood Glass factory at Lynn on 27 June 1974. The Princess, who was at the factory to officially open a £350,000 extension, had made several informal visits previously to see the ancient skills in action.

The Day The Floods Came

The floods of 1953, and to a lesser extent those of 1978, are the sort of events which lead people to say down the years, "What were you doing when...?"

For many families inundation spelled disruption and heartache, for some tragedy.

This evocative section brings together some poignant images of the consequences of Man underestimating Nature. Lynn now has an elaborate system of flood defences in place. But it is a brave, brave man who can say that Nature will not have the last word one day.

EDP reporter Frank Keeler got some first-hand experience of the gales when he visited Lynn Docks on that fateful January 1953 night.

A policeman gives advice to the crew of an ambulance trying to negotiate a flooded London Road.

The morning after: A mother and her baby are among occupants of a raft being towed through flooded South Lynn. No

...he high water mark of the floods, still clearly visible five or six feet above the ground on the walls of the houses.

Stranded householders in Portland Place can only look out of their first-floor windows and await the rescue raft

2 February and the *EDP* took to the skies to take these views of a Lynn still badly affected two days after the floods. At West Lynn, the Fropax factory is an island in a sea of floodwater, and in the streets of South Lynn the inundation is plain to see.

When the floods receded, the grim task of disposing of flood-damaged possessions began. Few people were insured; most lost everything at ground-floor level.

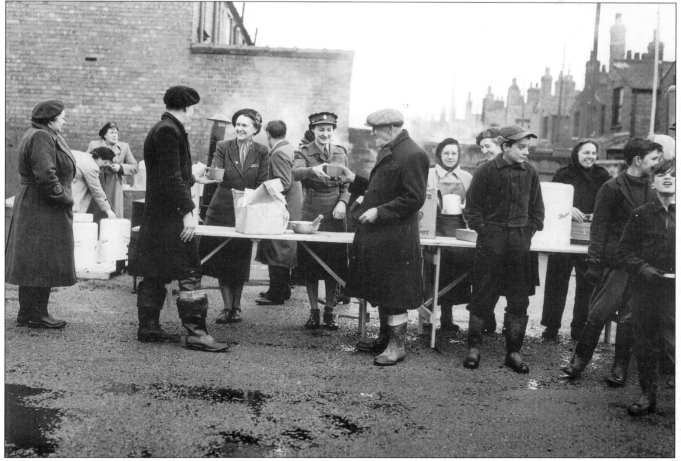

The cup that cheers: Time for a smile and a warming cup of tea as flood survivors swap their stories.

Windows flung open to try to dry their home out, the occupants of this South Lynn house remove their flood-damaged ground floor possessions.

A smile for the camera, but the shock is still there to see on the faces of these families. In the background, people queue for help and information at South Lynn Baptist Church, turned into a makeshift emergency centre.

The Queen leaves Gaywood Park Girls' School on 2 February 1953, after inspecting the emergency accommodation being provided there for flooded-out families.

Remembering… a civic procession makes its way through All Saints' Street, as part of a memorial service for the victims of the flood held on 18 February 1953.

11 January 1978, and the height of the flood surge can be judged by this dramatic view of the Saturday Market Place taken at the peak of the flooding. That's a Mini which lies almost submerged alongside the Town Hall.

Even this sturdy Land Rover needed a lookout to check for hazards ahead as it negotiated the waters.

Two legs good, four wheels bad… Shank's Pony proved a more reliable form of transport than many a car in Lynn on that night.

In an echo of scenes from 1953, rescuers ferry a stranded woman to safety in the Saturday Market Place.

The lower end of Lynn High Street, under more than a foot of floodwater. One youngster attempts to pedal his way out of trouble; his friend behind has given up the uneven struggle.

Will we get a second helping? That was the thought in the minds of these people at the Guildhall of St George in King Street as they await the next high tide.

Some unlucky residents have had floods on other dates as well as 1953 and 1978. The householders of this area of South Lynn had to put up with frequent inundations, such as this incident on 15 July 1968 – the second time in four days. The children might have enjoyed it, but for their parents it was no joke. One resident told how she had been flooded 27 times in just 15 years.

The day after: The Bishop of Lynn, the Rt Revd Aubrey Aitken, and the Revd Geoffrey Lang survey the waterlogged floor of St Margaret's Church on 12 January 1978. At its peak the flood had brought more than three feet of water into the church – worse than in 1953.

Lynn At Work ...

This section looks at some of the ordinary and extraordinary jobs Lynn people do. Running a mobile library van... or tunnelling under the Ouse, the *EDP* photographers are always there to capture the essence of the job with a memorable image.

Drink up, we deserve it... a celebration dram or two for workers after joining up the two halves of a tunnel under the Ouse on 11 June 1972. The 600-foot tunnel, 40 feet below the river, was built by teams of workers in shifts six days a week, 24 hours a day. The tunnel was built to service the new West Lynn sewage treatment works.

It was a case of three of a kind – or nearly – in this summer 1961 view of the Purfleet. The photographer spotted three different types of painter at work simultaneously – on the quayside, on the ship and working on the cupola of the Custom House. But during the time the plate camera was being set up the Custom House painter had stepped down from his ladder – and resolutely refused to go back up to complete the picture!

If you want to get a head… and another thirsty group of workers relax after a hard day. This showman and friend were enjoying a quick drink after preparing rides for the 1972 Lynn Mart. And didn't Lynn need a bit of fun, with power cuts, strikes and lay-offs grabbing the headlines locally and nationally. Fortunately the showmen were prepared – they brought their own generators.

This picture and the two following (see next page) are taken from a picture essay published in the *EDP* on 22 August 1952, when a photographer and reporter followed the crew of the *Rob-Pete* out of Lynn's Fisher Fleet for a day's cockling. Here skipper John Garnett (centre) and his crew repair the nets into which the shellfish were to be raked. Two of the fishermen can be seen raking the cockles from the Thief Sand in a race against the tides. The third picture shows the collected cockles being riddled to eliminate those which are undersized. The *Rob-Pete* – built by the famous Worfolk brothers – was converted back to a sailing craft in 1992 by actors Richard Heffer and Roy (Adam Dalgleish) Marsden.

The technique ancient, the setting decidedly modern... Bob Cleaver uses an old-fashioned seed fiddle to scatter grass seed over six acres of Hardwick roundabout on 15 May 1974. Contractors M.D.Pearce had tried various methods but decided the old ways were best.

It's 3.40pm on a December evening in 1967, and librarian Ron Bowyer is about to stamp the books of some visitors to the library van at St Peter's Road, West Lynn. Ron, who retired in 1993, set up the mobile library service in the Lynn area under chief librarian Mr Senior, and the Austin van quickly became a firm favourite around the town.

Shops and homes at Lynn had to turn to other sources of light and power in December 1970 when the town was hit by a power strike called by four unions in a pay dispute. Shops such as Halfords, pictured, tried to carry on as best they could. Meanwhile, the Eastern Electricity office at Wootton Road had its switchboard swamped by worried customers.

King's Lynn and District Wildfowlers lent a hand to help keep the Walks duck population in check in July 1971. Mike Etherington (right), the association's duck rearing officer, prepares to ring a mallard (being held by Terry Greenacre). The ducks were then taken to be re-released on the Snettisham reserve.

What's that then? That's been the question of many a summer visitor to Lynn's markets when confronted with their first sight of samphire, a true Norfolk delicacy. The bright green plant, also known as poor man's asparagus and by several other names is boiled or steamed and served with vinegar or melted butter. It only appears on market stalls for a few weeks in the summer and is quickly snapped up (the 1974 stall pictured had sold out, typically, by lunchtime). But, as the 1971 picture taken near the Point shows, gathering it is a messy, muddy business!

It used to be Bob-A-Job Week – but then along came decimalisation in 1971. So the renamed Scout Job Week was held instead. Here Cub Scout Tino Overson puts a fresh coat of paint on the shrimper *Susannah* in the Fisher Fleet in April 1971 for his task.

The Corn Exchange was the site for one of Lynn's busy markets every Tuesday morning. The specialist indoor farming market was held in tandem with the nearby cattle market, attracting farmers, seed merchants and agricultural machinery suppliers from a large area of West Norfolk, Marshland and South Lincolnshire. This 21 November 1952 picture shows plenty of bargains being struck at the building, which has now been converted into a multi-million pound entertainment complex.

Apt title: Pavior's mate Cliff Symed takes a break from his snow clearing duties in 1968, seemingly oblivious of the timely presentation at the Majestic Cinema behind him.

Valerie Dring gives a vote of thanks to guest of honour Mr J.O.Harrison at the King's Lynn Hospitals Management Committee School of Nursing presentation of awards on 12 July 1967. Watching her in the front row are, from left, Marion Bedford, Susan Woods (née Braybrooke), Sandra Russell (Fellowes), Anne Lemmon (Galloway) and Eileen Kittle (Hodson).

All in a day's work... the crew of the *Fertility* landed rather an unusual catch in January 1972 – a 500lb German acoustic mine. Fishermen Peter Yallop (left) and Jim ('Whiskers') Castleton found the bomb, complete with a large lobster living inside it. The device was later blown up outside Lynn, making a crater 40 feet deep and breaking windows as far away as Heacham.

Policeman Arthur Smith chats with Mrs Miller on the opening day of the new Lynn police station in June 1954.

Molten metal pours into a ladle as a furnace is tapped in the foundry at Cooper Roller Bearings on 28 February 1978. Cooper's celebrated its centenary in 1994 and its eventful first 100 years included making the bearings for the Jodrell Bank radio telescope – and producing its own car.

Now shall it be left or right? Decisions, decisions for council worker Mr R.W. Watkins of All Saints' Street, Lynn, whose job it was at the time of this May 1962 picture to remove experimental traffic signs on the Tuesday Market Place – and put them all out again every Tuesday and Saturday.

Ingenuity abounds in this March 1961 picture taken by an alert *EDP* photographer while walking down Broad Street. Catleughs Outfitters was one of the best-known family firms in Lynn. Its site is now taken by a health food store.

...And Lynn At Play

After being At Work it's time for play... and there is an equally wide range of ways Lynn people enjoy their leisure time. The chapter begins and ends with glimpses of the Walks, which has acted as the town's open-air leisure centre for more than two centuries.

The first really warm day of spring in 1969 was on 9 April... and what a perfect excuse for these Lynn characters to enjoy a spot of 'jawing' in the Walks.

Hat's a lot of fun: while their mums are busy in the 1966 Jermyn's sale, Rosemary Oliphant and Pamela Skipper take the chance to try out some of the bargains for themselves.

Your starter for ten… quizmaster Patrick Bowles asks another tricky question at the packed finals of the RAFA Top of the Town Quiz in 1966. The quiz was a regular fixture for would-be general knowledge kings for many years. In the 1966 finals, the Lynn Inspectors of Taxes 'B' team pipped Barclays Bank 35-23 thanks to a late surge.

June 1965, and Mrs M.Hartley (right) dispenses some advice at her flower arrangement class at the Lynn Tech.

Six-year-old Margaret Harris, her brother Andrew (next left), James Feeney and Susan Tucker with the new kinderbox at Lynn Public Library in November 1965. The box contained books chosen especially for young children.

A proud moment for these 1965 safe cycling award-winning Cub Scouts, pictured at Lower Canada, near the railway station. Town mayor Eddie Edgley (centre) can be seen with the recipients.

King's Lynn Town Band, pictured in November 1968 preparing for its fourth *Sounding Brass* concert with the Lynn Male Voice Choir. At the time this picture was taken, the band was reigning champion of East Anglia, a title it first won in 1954. The band celebrated its centenary in 1994.

Guy Fawkes' Night is one of the highlights of the year for any child (and, let's face it, for most of their parents too). This group of youngsters from the Loke were captured on film by the *EDP* building their bonfire on 1 November 1965. The presence of the camera was not welcomed by all the children, which led the paper to comment wryly: 'The youngster in the centre is not wearing a Guy Fawkes mask but giving a very good impression of one!'

Come on, you Lynn boys!... A crew of Lynn Sea Cadets bask in their victory over their Wisbech rivals in an Ouse rowing race in July 1963.

That's champion: All smiles from Lynn dock workers W.Mendham (holding cup) and G.Stephenson (with shield) in this late 1960s picture as they celebrated winning the National Dock Labour Board's South East Region First Aid awards.

Children + The Walks
= Fun – and these
youngsters, about to
sample the slide on a
September day in 1965,
were no exception.

Prize pet: Celebrations for
this top feline and its owner,
who had just won one of the
events at the North Lynn
fête in July 1968.

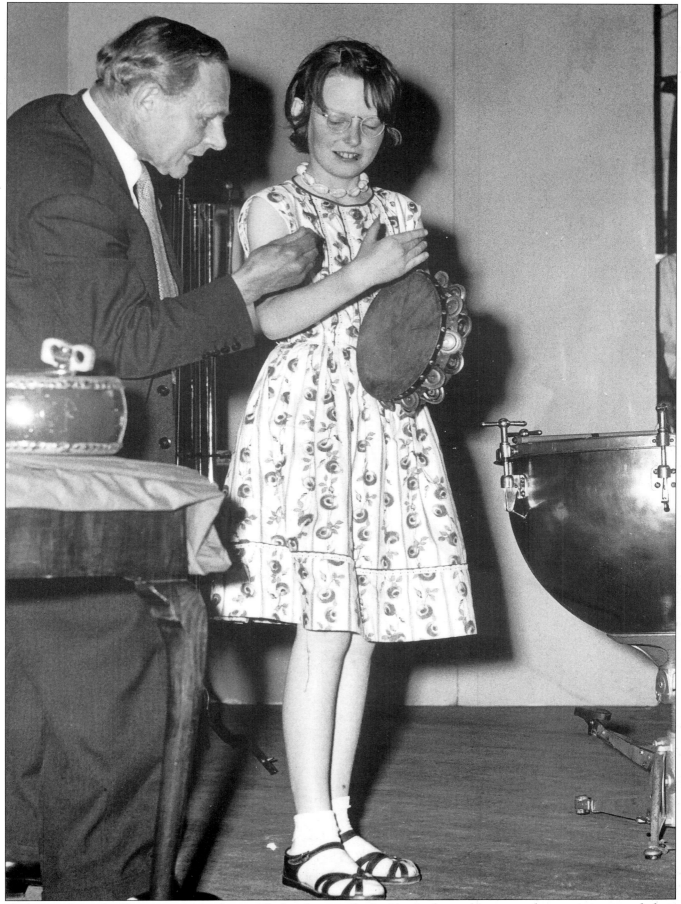

Shake, rattle and roll: Percussionist James Blades shows a junior Festival-goer how to make music at a workshop during the 1963 event.

Crowds at the North Guanock Gate in the Walks enjoy the unusual treat of a parade by the Royal Horse Guards on 25 July 1966.

Give us a ring… and that's just what these St Faith's ringers would do. Much in demand for carol concerts, the ringers – under the guidance of tower captain and Gaywood hairdresser Ernie Shipp – also used the handbells as a way of learning the art of bell-ringing proper. The ringers are seen practising in February 1967.

The Skating Royals
entertain the crowd at
a Lynn Round Table
Ball at the Corn
Exchange on 30
March 1961.

Generations of schoolboys
have had their first taste of
fishing along Lynn
waterfront. On a summer's
day in 1970, this youngster
is hoping to catch a 'flattie'
or two in the Fisher Fleet.

Grinning for the camera proved no problem for these children taking a break from their swimming exertions at the Walks open-air pool in September 1965.

Television presenter Keith Chegwin was besieged by 1,500 Lynn children when he brought the Saturday morning *Swap Shop* to the town centre on 10 February 1979. Cheggers interviewed Stars rider Michael Lee and Linnets player-manager Keith Rudd during the 20-minute live link.

The Lynn We Lost

Once Lynn's powers-that-be had taken the decision to go for expansion, the express train of redevelopment was the inevitable consequence. The immediate effect was the rapid speeding-up of the process, which began between the wars, of clearing crowded streets and yards and building new estates in places such as Gaywood. The old North End, the subject of a hotly-contested but unsuccessful preservation campaign, was first to go. Other areas followed, including many of Lynn's shopping streets. But much of the change was down to social changes and alterations in patterns of transport and industry. Rediscover long-lost views down streets which live on only in old street directories – and in people's hearts.

A view of Pilot Street in 1958 which is very different from today. The cottages on the chapel side of the street and St Nicholas' School seen here have since been demolished.

The demolition of Lynn's old North End was the first major post-war clearance scheme and a watershed in the town's recent history. This poignant 1958 view was taken from the rooftop of St Nicholas' Chapel. In the foreground St Nicholas' School, North Street, can be seen, and to the left a sign for Frank Castleton and Sons, fishing boat owners. In 1988 Frank Castleton published *Fisher's End*, an evocative and invaluable account of the fisher folk of Lynn. In the background of this picture the maze of streets off 'The Loke' can be seen.

Looking east along the old North Street. The flat roofed white building on the left was the yard of Frank Castleton, seen from a different angle in the top picture. Only True's Yard (now an acclaimed museum) remains as a tiny fragment of the old street and its cluster of yards.

St Ann's Street in 1958. The street has survived, but the businesses have changed. The Alexandra Dock Post Office was next to Southgate and Sons' store. The store's appeal to visiting sailors is shown by its Dutch sign Scheeps Handelaar. Southgate's other store, which was a few yards away in North Street, has been converted into the True's Yard site.

The ambitious expansion plans for Lynn in the 1960s included a complete revamp of its shopping and parking facilities to cater for the increase in population and to build on Lynn's traditional status as a regional centre. It was talk of the redevelopment of New Conduit Street which led to the *EDP* taking this now-historic picture in 1961.

The Employment Exchange, known as the Old Dole to workers there, can be seen on the left of this picture, again taken in the early 1950s. This part of the north side of the street also contained Horner's Music Shop and the Friends' Meeting House.

New Conduit Street had a range of family businesses and offices and many historic buildings. Number 21 was the Employment Exchange, and the *EDP* took this picture in the early 1950s to mark the refurbishment of its distinctive coat of arms.

Mrs Cawston's fruit and vegetable shop was boarded up by the time the *EDP* took this picture in 1969. The shop stood on the corner of Melbourne Street and South Clough Lane. The space between the houses on the right of the picture was caused by a bomb dropped in 1915 by a Zeppelin airship, one of the first air raids on British soil. The word 'clough' is an old Norfolk word for watercourse and rhymes with how – nothing to do with former football managers!

The compulsory purchase orders for the South Clough Lane area were published in May 1969, and soon the bulldozers were moving in (see opposite), leaving all or part of Bentinck Street, Blackfriars Street, Melbourne Street, Russell Place, Regent Street, South Clough Lane and St James' Road just a memory. The area is now a car park and the site for Lynn's St James' swimming pool.

Welwick House off All Saints' Street was one of the grandest casualties of Lynn's redevelopment. This July 1963 picture shows the once-proud house only a couple of years away from demolition. Mrs Lily Snasdell, whose newspaper shop was located in part of the building, said sadly on the eve of its destruction in May 1965: "I think it will break my heart when I have to go."

Lynn's old cattle market was a reminder every Tuesday of the rich rural hinterland which Lynn still dominates. It was also, as can be seen in this 1950s view, a splendid place for local children to meet animals at first hand.

March 1966, and another part of the old Hillington Square is cleared. Although the area had been earmarked for clearance as early as 1953 it was not until 1958 that a formal plan was considered by Lynn Town Council. An idea to build three tower blocks to replace the cleared houses was seriously considered for several years and was only dropped finally in the month this picture was taken.

Sad and forlorn, an empty Empire Cinema in Broad Street, which once echoed to the sounds of laughter of generations of pleasure-seeking Lynn people, is pictured in 1967 awaiting the bulldozers. Only the Majestic in Tower Street now remains in business as the last of Lynn's purpose-built cinemas.

It was vandals rather than developers who sealed the fate of one of the most unusual buildings in West Norfolk. The 18th-century Reffley Temple was sited near a spring at Gaywood. The Reffley Society, a group of local gentlemen, met here for hundreds of years, and the site was a popular picnic spot. Despite a 1789 curse warning vandals that they would die the last of their line if they defaced the buildings, the once-pretty site (pictured next page, top) was reduced to a sad pile of weeds and broken brick by the early 1980s.

Morgan's Ladybridge Brewery on the corner of Stonegate Street, pictured in April 1962. The brewery was cleared to make way for the Hillington Square flats development. The brewery's name was taken from the old Ladybridge Chapel which stood a few yards away, a fact which led local historian Henry Hillen to lament in 1907 'Alas, to what vile uses may the most sacred names be applied!'

The sheds at South Lynn Station, which was a casualty when the M & GN line closed for good in 1959. This picture was taken on 13 June 1958.

Dignity and pride was how the *EDP* headlined this picture of the sale ring at the now-redeveloped old Lynn Cattle Market in November 1965. The two-year-old shire fetched 67 guineas (£70.35), with the grey unsold. For market goers with a thirst, the Bird in Hand Tavern in Norfolk Street (rear entrance shown on the right of the picture) was one of many hostelries which catered for them.

The Windsor Road area was the next area of Lynn to be cleared, in October 1969. Properties – and whole streets – in Hospital Walk, Windsor Road, Keppel Street, Pleasant Row, Victoria Street, Wellington Street, Douro Street and Arthur Street disappeared.

Scott's Corner at the junction of Purfleet Street and High Street is no more as demolition work gets into full swing to level the department store in August 1971. The site is now occupied by the town's Boots store.

Not everyone was sad to see the old streets go. Mrs Annie Bunting watches as the Union Street house she had lived in for almost 30 years bit the dust in March 1968. She came back to see it because 'I just had to see it go'. Her previous next-door neighbour, Alan Gosling, was also there, carting the rubble away. "I always wanted to see it pulled down" he said.

School & College Days

The rapid expansion in Lynn brought large numbers of families with young children to the borough. That meant that educational facilities had to keep pace with the population changes too. So throughout the 1960s and 1970s new schools were built, Victorian buildings closed and older schools expanded. Lynn Technical College saw the foundations laid for the thriving centre for further education it is today. This chapter aims to capture some of these changes – but there's plenty of pictures, too, of children and students going about their day to day activities.

That first day at school is always special – and even more so when it's the first day of the school too. Fast-expanding Lynn saw several schools built to cater for the increased population. It's duffel-coat weather for youngsters at the South Wootton Infants School in April 1967 (top). Miss D.M.Roberts was the first headmistress of the school, helped by Mrs J.Hudson who was formerly a teacher at St James' Infants. The other picture shows the new Fairstead Junior Mixed and Infants School about to welcome its first pupils in September 1968. For four-year-old Charles O'Hara (left, with his mum) it was his first day at school; for Christopher (six) and Oliver Khoo (five), it was a switch from Howard School.

Welcome… and Lynn High School pupils greet guests arriving for the 1967 prizegiving at the Corn Exchange.

Making a splash: Enthusiastic trainee swimmers give their all at the opening of Alderman Catleugh Schools' pool on 1 July 1965. At the opening, by chairman of the governors Lord Romney, boys' school PE master Mr J.Lupson offered to run classes for parents too.

Clearly rather overawed, these pupils of Gaywood Primary School meet town mayor, Mr G.Gentle. Mr Gentle was paying a visit to six local schools on 27 May 1965 to mark Commonwealth Day.

Second-year general engineering students at Lynn Technical College discuss the finer points of the lathe with their instructor Mr A.Wilson (left). The students pictured on 4 May 1966 were Bob James, Alan Gooding, Keith Singer and Leonard Mowatt.

Elsewhere at the Tech, Mr K.H.Winson puts students through their paces in a French lesson at the language lab in March 1967.

All together girls... Concentration on their faces, pupils at King's Lynn High School get set for a musical contribution to their speech day at the Corn Exchange on 6 May 1965. Guest of honour, town mayor Eddie Edgley spoke of the 530 girls being crowded in the King Street premises and declared: "If ever any town needed a new school, King's Lynn needs a new high school for girls." A few years later, he got his wish.

Up… and over! A high jumper competes in the King Edward VII Grammar School sports day on 27 May 1965, against the unmistakable backdrop of the Edwardian building.

Come on! Encouragement and excitement on the faces of these Gaywood Primary School pupils and their parents at the school sports day on 22 June 1972.

Unseasonal blustery weather threatened to put a damper on the 1966 Alderman Catleugh Boys' School sports. But despite the wind and the rain, four records were broken, with 14-year-old Cameron Smith setting new marks in the weight and long jump events. Peter Barlow and Philip Pond were Victor Ludorum winners.

Under the careful supervision of instructor Mr Harman, Robin Edwards waits at a table in the old catering restaurant at Lynn Technical College on 19 May 1966. Mr Harman was teaching students the art of Silver Service Waiting. Among those enjoying their meal was lecturer Mr Downton (centre).

St Edmund's Junior School headmaster Mr Kingcome is raised on an hydraulic platform much to the amusement of his pupils on a visit to the new Lynn Fire Station near the school in October 1972.

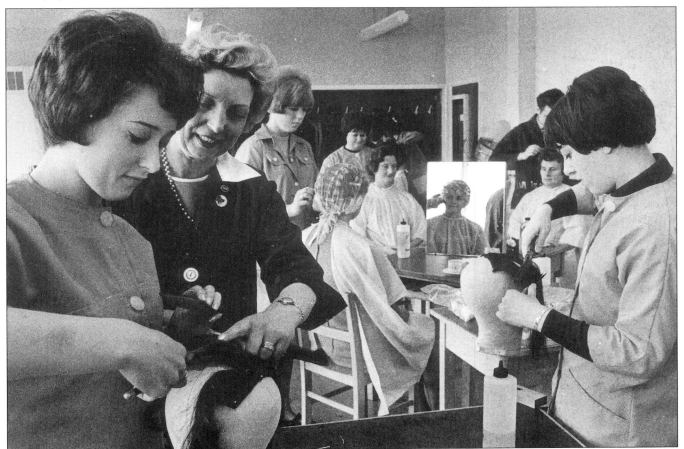

Hair today – a trade tomorrow... Students on Lynn Tech's new hairdressing course under the watchful eye of Mrs M.Eade (second left) in May 1966. The students also had to tackle art, science, English... and wig-making.

The Bishop of Northampton, the Rt Revd Charles Grant, visiting Gaywood in September 1967 to bless the £20,000 extension to the St Martha's RC School in Field Lane.

March 1974, and the 38 children of Class 3 in the infants department of West Lynn school had won one of the most sought-after possessions for a child growing up in the 1960s and '70s – a Blue Peter badge. The children, under the guidance of their teacher Miss Lesley Chapman, had written to the children's television programme as part of a class project. The staff at the show were so impressed with the pupils' efforts that the coveted badges were soon winging their way back.

St James' Boys' School had the first privately-built covered pool in Norfolk when it opened in November 1965. At its opening day, pictured here, headmaster Mr W.J.Baker paid tribute to the parents who had helped towards the £6,200 cost.

Pre-apprentice engineering students at work under Leslie Drinnan's keen gaze in the welding and sheet metalwork department at the technical college on 4 May 1966. The young students are Trevor Newstead, Tony Amos and John Farrow.

A break in rehearsals for a Gaywood Park School production of *Carousel* in November 1964.

It was him sir! and an accusing finger points to the author of a wrong note from the Alderman Catleugh School Band. The band, under the direction of music master Donald Ireson (seen having a word with the culprit) was rehearsing in May 1974 for a school concert.

It was the end of an era for two leading Lynn head teachers on 20 July 1972. Miss Diana Bullock (top), head of Gaywood Park Girls School since January 1952 – and one of Lynn's most passionate supporters of conservation – took her last class (poetry). And in another part of Gaywood, Harold Turner (right), head of Gaywood Primary for 19 years was also stepping down.

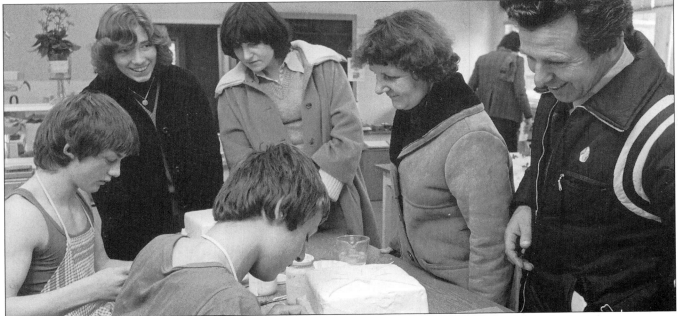

Two Gaywood Park pupils demonstrate to parents that culinary skills are not an exclusively female preserve at an open day in November 1978.

All Saints' School finally called it a day in May 1974. The school, which was more than a century old, was an infants and girls junior school until it amalgamated with St Margaret's Boys School in 1970. Once the site of the new Whitefriars School was fully ready, the old building was declared surplus to requirements and sold off. Mrs M.Cooper takes her final day's class at the old school.

Elizabeth Winder (left) and Susan Lewis created a quiet petticoat revolution in September 1978 when they ended the male-only tradition at King Edward VII School. The two teenagers – seen here with Jeremy Holmes and Stuart Coulden – joined the sixth form at KES. Just one year later the school became a full-fledged co-educational comprehensive.

Sporting Lynn

Lynn people have always loved their sport. And they've loved their football and speedway best of all. Here, then, are some nostalgic pictures for anyone who has ever stood on the terraces at the Walks or Saddlebow Road. The chapter includes the first-ever Stars meeting, plus pictures of such local sporting legends as Mick Wright and Terry Betts – and plenty of pictures of ordinary people enjoying the thrill of competing at their chosen sport.

Shale and hearty: A huge crowd of 5,500 greeted the first outing for the new King's Lynn Stars at their Saddlebow Road debut on 24 May 1965. Having risen from the ashes of the Norwich Stars, Lynn Stars provided 30 years of speedway action until 1995. In that first meeting, Terry Betts came out of retirement to gain maximum points.

Practice days have always been a great way for speedway fans to get an informal view of their favourite riders – and see those machines in close-up. Here fans meet a rider at a late 1960s session.

Terry Betts, then co-holder of the World Best Pairs title and regular in the British team, put his considerable expertise at the disposal of 16 would-be speedway riders in a training school at Saddlebow Road in November 1972. Here he is passing on some advice to one of the riders.

They're off! Engines roar as riders get off to a flying start at an England versus Australia match at Saddlebow Road. The stadium has seen many fine international meetings – including this one in July 1973 when England (with the help of Terry Betts and Malcolm Simmons) came from behind to beat the Aussies 44-34.

Matches between Lynn Stars and Ipswich Witches have always had an extra edge, bringing together the traditional rivalry of Norfolk and Suffolk. In this British League Division One clash on 16 August 1972, it was Lynn who took the spoils. Stars Phil Crump and Terry Betts lead Ipswich's Sandor Levai into a bend.

Seeing Stars: Lynn's Howard Cole receives attention after he had been forced to come off his machine to avoid a fallen Newport rider at the club's 15 June 1969 meeting.

Terry Betts was the great stalwart of the Stars during their early years – and captain when this March 1976 team picture was taken. But waiting in the wings was someone who was to top even Betts' proud record – Michael Lee. Lee, seen fourth left in back row, started rewriting the record books a year earlier when he became the youngest rider – at just 16 – to score a paid maximum in the first division. In fact he was already the veteran of 120 meetings for Stars and Boston when he lined up up for the *EDP* cameras. Lee told the paper his ambition was to be world champion 'as soon as possible' – in the event, he had to wait four more years. For the record, this 1976 line-up was (back row) manager Alan Littlechild, Jan Heningsen, David Gagen, Lee, Adi Funk (front) Roy Bales, Betts and Ian Turner.

David Ladbrook jockeys his ski-board over the wake from the tow launch during an evening's water-skiing on the Ouse on 1 July 1970.

No football club could ask for a better servant than Mick Wright, seen here in 1970. After joining the Linnets from Northampton in October 1961, Wright notched up a British senior record of 1,152 appearances for Lynn, playing in virtually every position in the team. A hero off the pitch too; he hit the headlines in 1991 for saving a man from drowning on Lynn's waterfront.

It was a case of Linnets v Bloaters in May 1966 when Lynn met Great Yarmouth at the Walks in the Norfolk Invitation Cup Final. The large crowd saw the Linnets (Walls, Haskins, Sharp, Brooks, Porter, Wright, Bacon, Chilleystone, Lindsay, Laverick, Banson) go behind in the 24th minute – hence these anxious looks from the fans – but Linnets stalwarts Lindsay and Wright secured the cup for West Norfolk with a goal apiece.

Vere Hodson was a familiar face at the Walks stand in the late 1960s. His claim to fame was as Lynn FC's oldest supporter. Vere, who lived in nearby Tennyson Avenue, was 95 when this picture was taken at a match against Hillingdon. He was usually accompanied by his great-grandsons David, Michael and Andrew.

1967 was a good year for junior Lynn soccer – no fewer than five of the town's schoolboys were called up for the county squad. Celebrating for the *EDP* are Peter Morris (KES), Nicholas Brett (Ald Catleugh), John Bushrod, Timothy Maxwell and Daniel Serella (all Gaywood Park).

In these days of seemingly year-round football, it seems hard to remember than only a few years ago the close season was counted in months and not days. For the Linnets the end of the close season in 1967 began on 18 July, when the players were put through their paces for a evening training session around the Loke Road area.

Linnets manager Len Richley discusses tactics with his squad in November 1964 on the eve of their (unsuccessful) FA Cup first-round trip to Shrewsbury. Pictured listening are, back row from left, Gerry Baker, Mick Wright, Roy Proverbs, Bob Edwards, Jack Walls, and (front row) Barrie Jones, Bobby Laverick, David King, David Partridge, Roy Banham, Ian Williamson and Ronnie Bacon. Wright and Bacon were the only survivors of the Lynn side which played mighty Everton in the celebrated January 1962 Cup-tie.

Lynn Friars boxing club, founded in the 1950s, followed in the footsteps of the Lynn Regis club to give expert coaching to local youngsters wanting to take up 'the noble art'. The *EDP* pictured club members at their Ferry Street site in the late 1960s including secretary Harry Temby (left), David Hemming (fourth left), Stefan Wasinack, Gary Knight (fourth right), John Twell (with paintbrush) and Peter Yallop (right).

At the time of this September 1968 picture, speedway was all the craze at Lynn... cycle speedway, that is. Loke Road and Harding's Pits were popular venues for this informal summer sport. This picture was taken at a keenly-contested derby between South Lynn and North Lynn Aces. The North won.

The Milk Race came to Lynn in May 1977 bringing 60 of the finest international cyclists – and a massive media circus in tow. Poland's Ryszard Szurkowski wore the leader's jersey as the riders set off from the Albert Street car park for the 101-mile stage to Leicester. Among the spectators at Lynn was a real cycling fan – pop idol Alvin Stardust.

West Norfolk Rugby Club, led by captain Mike Credland, playing a Midlands and East Anglia side in September 1974 to start off the club's golden jubilee season in style. The North Wootton-based club hosted Ken Chapman, president of the Rugby Football Union, to the match. But the visitors were not in generous mood; they won 44-12.

On the oche: one of the lady darts players involved in the Watney Mann's pub sports finals aims for the bull on 4 May 1971. Players competed at both darts and dominoes at the finals, held in the Corn Exchange.

The new indoor pool gave a boost to efforts to launch a water polo league in West Norfolk. A club at the St James' Pool soon had 35 members – and two of them are seen at a training night in August 1976 – with John Youngman as captain.

KES' under-15 cricket team made Norfolk sporting history in 1975 when they became what was believed to be the first county school to reach the final of a national sporting competition. The team were off to the Oval for the final of the Lords Taverners Trophy against holders Radley College. The team, from back, Chris Nelson, Mike Pounder, Ian Oakes, Steve Bunting, Keith Hawkins, Ray Howard (middle row) Bill Hooker, Doug Killick, Pat Cooke, Richard Bird, (front row) Ian Grady, scorer Richard Cross and Mark Fuller, found the champions just too strong, losing out by 44 runs.

Liquid refreshment for two members of the victorious Glamorous Linnets team who took on King's Lynn Nurses in a charity football match at the West Norfolk Fertiliser's sports pitch in September 1965. Kicked off by local long-distance walker Bob Thirtles, the match saw Ann Ebbs score five goals for the Linnets.

Back In Time, Gentlemen Please

Lynn's pubs may have sharply declined in number since the early 1950s – the numbers of licences has fallen by almost two-thirds – but they still play an important social role in the town's life.

This brief section shows a selection of locals visited by the *EDP* cameras over the years.

Borough mayor Fred Juniper pulled the first pint at the new Wildfowler pub off Gayton Road in April 1976. The Ansells pub was a £57,000 conversion of the old Fairstead farmhouse. Managed by Mr and Mrs Michael Goodman, the pub's name was chosen from more than 500 possibles in a competition.

Barmaid Mrs Mabel Hitch was a veteran of four Lynn pubs when she finally called it a day, at Fiddaman's Hotel in Norfolk Street on 26 March 1965. Seen here receiving a presentation by members of the pub's social club, she told the *EDP* the secret of being a good barmaid: "You must have a sense of humour, a broad mind and a sympathetic ear," she said.

The Grosvenor pub, on the corner of Norfolk Street and Broad Street, closed its doors for the last time in August 1969 – the ninth Lynn pub to close in a year, sharing the fate of the neighbouring Fiddaman's Hotel which had been demolished and redeveloped earlier in the decade. The Grosvenor was thought to have dated from the 1740s.

Not all 1960s pub stories were of closures. Maid's Head Hotel landlord Colin Atkinson (pictured right) invited borough mayor and mayoress Mr and Mrs John Juby to open its dance hall in August 1966. The hall featured low tables, subdued lighting and a blue and orange decor. Mr Juby defended his visit to a pub. "Some people may frown on the mayor and mayoress going into public houses in a public capacity, but we look upon them as playing an important part in the social life of the town," he told the *EDP*.

Lynn MP Derek Page gets set to give fundraisers a bit of a push – by demolishing a pile of pennies collected by regulars at the Golden Ball in Tower Street on 20 January 1970.

The More Things Change ...

...the more they stay the same, or so the saying has it. And certainly there are many views in this selection showing various areas of Lynn which have stayed much the same to this day. But take a closer look, and even these familiar views show the changes wrought over the years.

Still bearing the scars of the wartime bombing which badly damaged adjoining Boal Street, this late 1940s picture shows Greenland Fishery, once a whaling inn, then a museum. The Society for the Protection of Ancient Buildings recommended in December 1945 that this 'most interesting and picturesque structure' be saved. Fortunately for succeeding generations of Linnets, it was.

The Littlewoods store in High Street receives a civic opening from Lynn mayor Harold Birdseye, seen here flanked by eager shoppers. The new store, which opened in November 1970, was typical of the big-name multiples which changed the face of Lynn shopping in the 1960s and 1970s. Key Markets had opened in the redeveloped New Conduit Street the previous year, and 1970 would see the opening of a new-look Tesco too.

A quiet moment at what is now one of Lynn's busiest traffic spots, the South Gates roundabout. As the volume of traffic has increased, the roundabout has shrunk to try and speed traffic flow. The Ford garage and Southgates filling station have also changed since this 1962 picture, but the magnificent southern gateway to Lynn still dominates the area as it has done since 1520.

The Lynn police station, seen here at its 1954 opening, was the biggest single development since the Lynn Borough Police was founded in 1835. One fascinating might-have-been in Lynn history is that this very corner was looked at by leisure entrepreneur Ben Culey in 1938 as the site for a massive 1,242-seater cinema which would have been called The Regal.

Very few businesses have survived to the present day from this 1957 view of upper High Street. The Wenn's Hotel (left) and Jermyn's (now Debenham's) remain but the Kettering and Leicester Boot Company has gone, as has the Cheshire Cheese pub.

Hampton Court off Nelson Street is one of Lynn's great architectural treasures. But when this early 1950s picture was taken, its future was not so sure. By the end of the war the once-proud building was divided int tenements and needed extensive restoration, but its luc turned when Mrs E.A.Lane of Holbeach bought th

operty for £800 in 1953. She began improvements, and nded over two wings of the building to the Lynn Civic ciety (and its offshoot Lynn Preservation Trust) to restore. By 1962 the work was complete at a cost of around £50,000.

Foundations proceed apace for the new arcade of shops in New Conduit Street in the late 1960s. In the background, the old Broad Street is rapidly being levelled.

15 September 1969, and the old Sedgeford Lane is virtually gone. Rising in its place is the spiral ramp which leads t

After months of traffic delays, Lynn finally saw its new Freebridge open on 16 December 1970. An army team had built a 500-foot temporary bridge for traffic a year earlier while the work was carried out.

he rooftop New Conduit Street car park.

It's hard to believe that only a few years ago, rail was still king along the South Quay. In 1962 when this picture was taken rail sidings extended all the way along to the Boal Quay. Now early-bird commuters flock to the quay every morning to take advantage of free parking.

Le Grice Bros – seen here in November 1962 – was one of Lynn's leading stores. Next to their premises, bought by Tesco in 1967, was WH Smith. Heading towards Foster's Corner are Hepworth's and Hilton's shoes. Opposite Le Grice's was MacFisheries.

This December 1961 view of Union Lane, alongside Jermyn's, includes a view of one of the earliest branches of electrical store Wheelers, which became one of West Norfolk's best-known family businesses.

Rivetts of Lynn had two High Street stores, number 77 and – pictured on 3 October 1960 – number 51. Staff pictured here included Pansy Hazel (behind counter), Dinah Shackcloth (demonstrating the knitting machine) and Angie Beeken on the stepladder.

Taken in December 1961, the *EDP* camera looked along St James' Street from the Saturday Market Place. The handsome sign of the White Hart Stores can be seen on the left, and other well-known names include County Electrical Services, Dennis and Son butchers ('Dennis's Celebrated Pork Pies') and, at the far distance, the former Rummer pub.

Squeezing between the traffic was an occupational hazard for shoppers in the High Street. On this April day in 1962, they were visiting familiar names such as Smiths Cleaners, Purdys, Dolcis, Easiephitt, Rivetts... and, of course, the *Eastern Daily Press*.

Flowerpot Corner on the junction of Norfolk Street and Chapel Street – from where this picture was taken in September 1965 – was the site of numerous scrapes between cars negotiating their way around Lynn's narrow shopping streets.

For more than 240 years the Walks have given Linnets the chance to enjoy a taste of the countryside a few minutes from town. This 1953 shot shows the bandstand, paddling pool and open-air swimming pool, which was opened in 1921 and closed in the late 1970s.

Although some of the names in the St James' Street businesses seen on the right of this picture may have changed, the beauty of the Tower Gardens remains a much-loved quiet corner of the town centre. This 1959 picture shows work preparations for the summer display of flowers.

A rainy day in April 1957, and a busy scene in the High Street is captured for posterity. Well-known names pictured include the Trustees Savings Bank and the Café Imperial. Just visible on the right, at the end of the arch, is the now-demolished Queen's Head pub.

Pedestrianisation was still years away when these cars and a cyclist went down Norfolk Street in April 1962.

What to do about Lynn's traffic problems had been vexing planners since at least 1948. Getting cars out of High Street, Broad Street and New Conduit Street was one priority – pedestrianisation started gingerly with an experimental Saturday ban. These September 1965 High Street shoppers enjoy their new freedom.

Framingham Almshouses are one of several almshouses which still survive in Lynn, a relic of the pre-Welfare State philanthropists of bygone years. This October 1959 picture includes resident Arthur Asker (left) on his doorstep enjoying the autumn sunshine.

The shape of things to come – 16 April 1971, and pens on Lynn Cattle Market are removed to increase car parking space next to the central area. Only a few months later the whole market had transferred to its new site, and removal of the old market began in earnest.

Paul Hawkins, later Sir Paul, joins workers at the new Hardwick Narrows cattle market for a traditional topping-out pint in June 1971.

Going... going... gone – and another Lynn landmark vanishes, with the demolition of the 134-foot chimney at the Fison's plant at Saddlebow Road, South Lynn, in April 1973. The reporter wrote: 'She may not have been very attractive standing up but it looked very graceful falling down, with an explosion which would have made Guy Fawkes green with envy.' At least one person was glad to see it come down – security officer Mr R.Bennington whose unenviable job in earlier years at the old 'Muck Works' had been been to climb the chimney on maintenance duties.

George Emery prepares to attack the iron shell of the old Kettle Mill at Lynn in April 1972. The Kettle Mill once supplied Lynn with water, with the flow of the Gaywood River pumped into an upper tank and then gravity-fed through the town. Local fishermen were sad at the mill's demise; they used it as a landmark when returning from the Wash.

Of Lynn's three great Victorian engineering firms, Savage, Dodman's and Cooper's, sadly only the latter now remains. But before its demise in 1975, there was a time when Alfred Dodman and Co's name was known all over the world. The Highgate works (seen here in 1971) helped pioneer steam power for farming and turned out products ranging from gold mining machinery for South Africa to water installations in India.

The Rowlinson and Lowton-Cubitt system-built homes on estates such as North Lynn helped speed up the pace of house building to meet the growth in the borough's population in the 1960s. The *EDP* spotlighted local mothers Mrs Marion Andrews and Mrs Pauline Andrews, and cousins Julie, Bonnie and Sherie Andrews at Chadwick Square in November 1966.

Eleven-year-old Michael Clarke helps Christine Hooks, ten, plant a cherry tree along Columbia Way, North Lynn. They were two of 42 St Edmund's Junior School children who planted saplings on this day (23 February 1966).

Left: The clock tower of the Majestic dominates this view of the southern end of Tower Street taken on 21 March 1969, just as it does today. The properties to the right of the picture were soon to be demolished as part of the New Conduit Street redevelopment.

Below: Michael Shepherd (left) and Jack Brown pulling slates from the R1, R2 and R3 warehouses at Alexandra dock on 2 May 1972, as their demolition work gets under way. The six-storey Victorian buildings had been damaged by fire and deemed unsuitable for modern freight movements. Their last tenant, East Anglian Grain, had moved out three years earlier.

Bottom: For more than 60 years the beet sugar factory at Saddlebow dominated the skyline south of Lynn, employed hundreds of local people and poured millions into the West Norfolk economy. This October 1970 study shows the distinctive plume of steam as the beet campaign gets into full swing.

Entertainment

A look at some more of the ways Lynn people like to entertain – and be entertained. The chapter includes scenes from Lynn's famous appearance before millions of television viewers in the BBC's zany *It's A Knockout* programme.

The Corn Exchange was the venue for a Festival Beat Concert in 1966, starring the Honeycombs – seen here with some young fans – and vocal duo Mikki and Griff.

A jumbo attraction in every way... It's 1966 and a free show for these delighted youngsters and their parents as elephants from Sir Robert Fossett's Circus make their way to the Walks big top.

Jack Bodger congratulates Pauline Griffin, of South Wootton, and Ann Button, who were chosen to represent King's Lynn in the Eastern Region Hospitals Personality Girl contest in February 1965.

King's Lynn Operatic and Dramatic Society chose their most ambitious project for 14 years when they staged the romantic melodrama *New Moon* in March 1966. With Walter Rye (left foreground) and John Blair (right) as male leads, the Willie Martin-produced play involved no fewer than 185 period costumes – and 65 wigs. Suzanne Webborn was the leading lady.

A handshake by borough mayor Mr A.E.Panks for Manchester's deputy Lord Mayor began a night of fun and mayhem on 22 April 1973, when *It's A Knockout* came to town. The Tuesday Market Place, packed with 3,000 spectators, was the venue for the Lynn v Manchester heat of the popular television show. Presenters Eddie Waring and Stuart Hall compered the contest, later watched by millions of viewers, which was won by Manchester by 12 points, winning the side a place in an international heat in Switzerland.

Some of the members of the cast of Benjamin Britten's *Noye's Fludde*, one of the most ambitious productions involving local schoolchildren staged in the 1960s. Two performances at St Margaret's Church in October 1965 played to appreciative audiences.

Flying high… capturing the sensation of a Mart ride on camera calls for a steady hand – and a strong stomach – as amply demonstrated in this dizzying 1971 view, while the 1973 fair gave the chance for a more reflective shot with a Mart-goer framed against the big wheel.

Members of the local police force discovered a beat of a different sort in 1972 when they formed the pop group Treble 9. The group comprised station sergeant George Hooke (organ), PC Derek Stuart of Litcham (lead guitar), DC Ron Elliott of Lynn CID, PC Trevor Bidle of Lynn (rhythm guitars), PC Michael Hayman (bass) and PC Chris Naylor on drums. The group was formed in March and by May was auditioning for an appearance on television talent show *Opportunity Knocks*.

Ten little fingers, ten little toes... Some of the more junior members of the Pat West School of Dancing go through their paces for the *EDP* cameras in May 1972.

Front Page News

King's Lynn has had more than its fair share of dramas over the years ... and the *Eastern Daily Press* has been there to record them.

But away from the fires and the rescues there is also the occasional offbeat event which also makes the headlines.

You've never had it so good... and that was certainly the enthusiastic reception King's Lynn gave to Prime Minister Harold Macmillan in October 1959. 'Supermac' was greeted by a cheering 2,000-strong crowd as he began the first leg of a whistle-stop tour of East Anglia at Lynn during that year's General Election campaign.

Kim the black labrador found himself in the news after taking an early morning dip in the Ouse on 28 May 1971. Passers-by noticed he couldn't get out, prompting sea cadets from the TS *Vancouver* to row a boat round to the Purfleet to keep the dog in the creek until help arrived, in the shape of Trevor Funnell. The reporter added: 'On the bank Kim did the usual things all dogs do – he stood near to as many people as possible and shook himself dry, drenching everyone.' Ungrateful hound!

Several hundred shoppers and office workers gathered in King Street on 30 November 1965 to witness a fire at the Freebridge Rural District Council offices. Retained fireman R.C.Chase, from the nearby Common Staithe station, was hurt after falling through a fire-weakened ceiling.

Not loafing around: This was the scene outside the Hot Bread Kitchens in the Vancouver Centre in early December 1974. The reason? Bakery workers had gone on strike, creating panic among housewives up and down the country. Lynn bakeries reported their shelves cleared by 10am – stocks of flour, yeast and even rye crispbreads ran low too.

This push-me, pull-you Mini had the traffic wardens scratching their heads in Lynn in January 1971. The car was built by a Lincolnshire man from the remains of two scrapped cars, and proved an attraction at the Mann Egerton showrooms in Church Street.

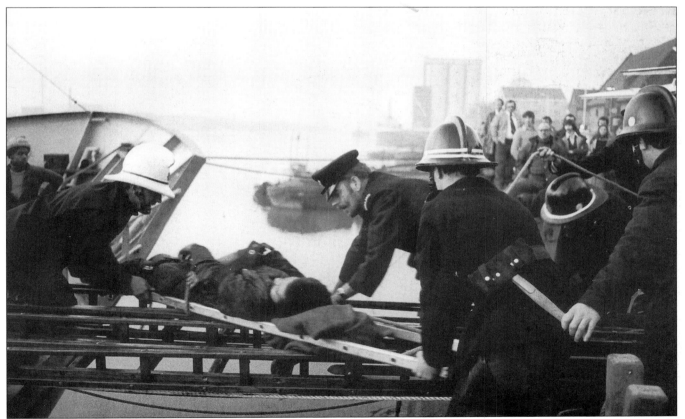

Firefighters had to act quickly on 6 February 1975 when two Dutch seamen were overcome by carbon monoxide fumes as their ship berthed at the South Quay. Using aluminium ladders, fire crew using breathing apparatus rescued the two men. With darkness falling, they used one of the ladders as a makeshift stretcher to get the seamen on to dry land – and safety.

So the last Hunstanton train ran on 3 May 1969? No, not quite. The line might have closed for passenger traffic on that date, but the very last trains ran in March and April 1971. A shunting engine gradually headed back to Lynn station, the crew dismantling the line as it went along, effectively ending hopes of re-opening the route. The *EDP* wrote that the line was 'on the threshold of being just a memory'.

Unfortunately even King's Lynn Football Club was not immune to the sort of scenes which plagued bigger and more famous clubs in the 1970s and 1980s. This dramatic picture shows one of several arrests at the FA Cup-tie between the Linnets and then non-League Wimbledon on 24 November 1973. The 65th-minute winning goal was scored by Lynn's Elliott, but for many of the 2,000-plus fans the violence had taken the shine off the victory.

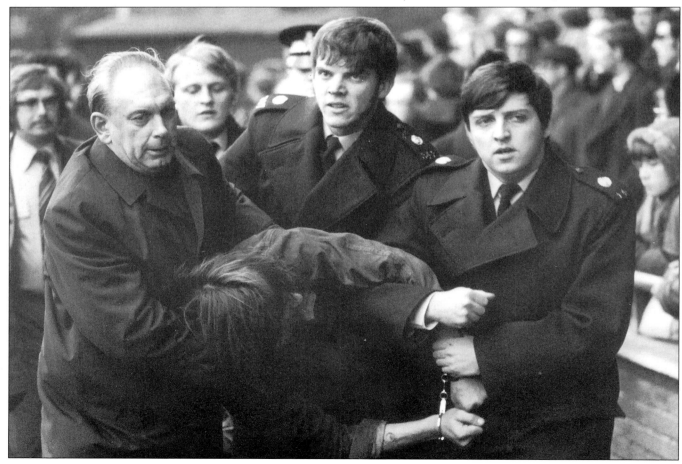

The Red Mount Chapel saw one of the most colourful events in its 400-year history in 1968, when all Lynn's churches got together to reopen the chapel as an interdenominational place of worship. Town mayor Mr H.C.Simpson symbolically handed the keys to the Bishop of Northampton, the Rt Revd Charles Grant, who handed them in turn to the other clergy. Seven hundred people watched the historic open-air service.

Not even an distinctly unseasonal snow shower (this was 2 June 1975) could stop the determined mums of pupils of Whitefriars School in their campaign for better road safety for their children. The mothers, led by Angela Brock, Olive Francis and Yvonne Todd, held their protest march every day for well over a year until something was done.

More fire drama, this time in Lynn High Street. Window cleaner Ken Sharman and caretaker Mr S.A.Juby were heading for work at 6.30am on 12 June 1968 when they noticed wisps of smoke coming from the International store. Within a few minutes the first of four fire engines arrived – and spent more than five hours tackling the blaze. More than £10,000 worth of stock was damaged by fire and water.

Ancient and modern: A Lynn council macebearer stands on Tuesday Market Place as Canberras and Victor tankers from RAF Marham fly past. The picture was taken during the conferring of the Freedom of the Borough on the air base to mark many decades of friendship. Thousands of people turned out on 6 December 1976 to witness the pomp and ceremony.

Some of the 8,000-strong crowd at a Lynn Knockout contest scatter as gusty conditions blow a hot-air balloon towards them at the June 1972 event. After several attempts, the decision was taken to abandon the balloon flight. Fifteen teams took part in the Round Table-organised event, which raised £1,200 for charity.

The picket line at Lynn fire station on the first day of the national firefighters' strike on 14 November 1977. Soon Army Green Goddesses were as common a feature in the streets of West Norfolk as in other towns up and down the country.

This steel silo, containing 500 tonnes of beans, collapsed on 9 October 1972 while a ship was being loaded at the South Quay. Lynn docker Stan Griffin had a lucky escape – he was just 20 feet away when the silo began to buckle.

Around 5.10pm on 27 June 1976, the unthinkable happened – an explosion at Dow Chemical. The blast ripped through part of the plant with a force equal to 300lbs of TNT, sending a mushroom cloud hundreds of feet into the air and scattering debris over a wide area. This exclusive *EDP* picture captures the scene just minutes after the blast as fire crews tackled the aftermath. The explosion cost the life of a factory firefighter and caused £1.25 million worth of damage.

The View From The Top

Aerial views of Lynn have always been a popular feature of the EDPs news pages. And, naturally, the wider the area covered in the picture the quicker the scene will change, guaranteeing almost instant nostalgia. The huge scale of the changes in street patterns since the 1950s can be fully seen too. The chapter includes a bird's eye view with a difference!

The launch of Anglia Television gave an unexpected chance for a series of classic aerial shots of Lynn. Before the station went on air on 27 October 1959, a helicopter toured the transmission area for publicity purposes. When it arrived at Lynn, the *EDP* took the chance to take this splendid picture.

A poignant view of pre-development Lynn on 1 September 1959. To the left is the cattle market (now Sainsbury's car park) and the old Broad Street leads off to the Post Office. The tree-lined New Conduit Street leads to the distinctive 1930s façade of Burton's. And behind the shopping streets is a cluster of warehouses and yards.

Another view from that 1959 flight. The camera was over King Edward VII Grammar School looking west when this picture was taken. The new Tech dominates the picture, but also of interest is the old Highgate 'village in a town' at the top of the picture which was being redeveloped.

Queen Mary Road sweeps elegantly down to the top left of this 1959 picture, which graphically shows some of the hundreds of homes built in Gaywood from the 1930s as clearances in the heart of Lynn moved much of the population out to the suburbs. Gaywood formally ceased to be a separate village in 1935, but changing social patterns and easier transport had started the process long before.

R.G.Carter worker Trevor Hand had an unusual view of the bustling Tuesday Market Place on one of its busiest days of the year in mid-May 1974. Mr Hand was taking a break from painting the exterior of the Duke's Head Hotel.

A few months earlier, an *EDP* photographer had flown over Lynn to take this view of the Purfleet. The old and the new are contrasted; in the foreground a grain ship berthed (attracting the attention of a flock of swans). T

the right is the elegance of King's Staithe Square and the other side is the Custom House. In the background the spiral roadway to the New Conduit Street rooftop car park is a symbol of changing Lynn.

Putting the finishing touches to the restoration of Lynn's Greyfriars Tower in May 1973. The new Hillington Square flats can be seen in the background – plus a couple of the buses waiting for passengers in the Fleet.

Looking south from the Norfolk College main block over the Walks in July 1973. In the middle of the picture is the former Lynn maltings (now converted into flats) and beyond the Walks the tower at Campbell's can be seen.

A darkening sky gives a suitably dramatic air to this view over Lynn looking west from the top of the newly-completed main block at Norfolk College in 1973. In the foreground Highgate, while on the horizon the Saddlebow beet sugar factory, Paul's Mill and St Margaret's Church dominate the skyline.

A tower crane at Lynn docks was the vantage point for this 1970 view of St Ann's Street and St Nicholas' Chapel. Since this picture was taken, many of the buildings seen at the corner of St Nicholas' Street and Chapel Street have been cleared.

A 1959 photograph of Lynn's Alexandra Dock. The timber trade which is still a large part of the ports trade is much in

evidence here, as is the once-extensive network of rail sidings.

Lest we forget… and the top of Greyfriars Tower provided an unusual perspective on the 1978 Remembrance Day ceremony at Tower Gardens.

The 140-foot high Paul's Mill chimney on the Boal Quay survived the demolition of the rest of the site for the best part of two decades because of its usefulness as a training site for steeplejacks. It was first used for this purpose in 1977 by these trainees on a course run on behalf of the Federation of Steeplejacks by the Construction Industry Training Board at Bircham Newton.

Bird's eye view: A huge flock of starlings dominate the familiar skyline of St Nicholas' Chapel on 27 September 1972.

A splendid view of the Tuesday Market Place in September 1962 with the parked cars making a pleasing geometric pattern when seen from on high.

People (And Their Pets, Too)

'News is People', wrote the great newspaper editor Harold Evans in 1963. 'It is people talking and people doing.'

So one of the essential skills of being a press photographer is to get right to the heart of the story to bring out that human element. And, come to think of it, sympathy for people as subject matter applies equally well to their pets...

Every dog has his day – and the splendidly-named Josoto Capability Brown of Trapagaz had his in February 1975. The poodle was pictured being groomed for an appearance at Cruft's, displayed by his proud owner Mrs C.Flatt of Pets' Paradise, Tower Street. The grooming procedure involved preening, washing – and the judicious use of curlers.

A chance walk down Priory Lane in the early 1960s resulted in this charming study for the *EDP*. Elizabeth Knowles reads to her granddaughter Bobbie watched by neighbour Mrs Allen.

Rosebery Avenue resident Mrs Edith Parsons, 90, receives an Easter gift from children at the Gaywood school in March 1977. The Rosebery Avenue First School pupils had saved their pocket money to buy treats for 50 local pensioners.

A modern Lynn tradition enjoyed by hundreds of pensioners is the annual Shallow Tea named after benefactor George Shallow, who left a legacy so that older people in the borough could have 'a little bit of something extra at Christmas'. The result – a meal in the Town Hall every autumn. This 1974 Shallow Tea was attended by 200 people.

Going up… and King's Lynn magician Graham Wilson and his wife Hazel demonstrate their levitation trick in a then topical (c.1967) reference to the soon-to-rise Hillington Square flats development behind them. Graham began his career when he was ten, and Mr and Mrs Wilson toured all over the world in their globe-trotting career. And Graham is still entertaining the people of West Norfolk through his alter ego as Jingles the clown.

Judge Frederick Beezley (left) leads Judge Adrian Head and Judge David Moylan at the annual judges' service on 8 October 1978 at St Margaret's Church.

Man is a dog's best friend: When his 14-year-old mongrel Sally got too old for her daily constitutional, 76-year-old Percy Powley of Anderson Close hit upon the perfect solution – take her for bike rides instead. Percy told a reporter in February 1975: 'She's too old to run around now, but she still likes me to take her down to the Walks every day. I used to take her to the pub every night – until she got past it.'

Seven-year-old Helen Hornigold and her brother James, three (pictured right), at a jumble sale they organised and ran outside their Cresswell Street home in August 1970. The children were raising money to buy a kidney unit for Lynn hospital.

7 June 1977 was the day Lynn joined the rest of the United Kingdom in celebrating the Queen's Silver Jubilee in style. This party at Beloe Crescent, South Lynn, was one of no fewer than 40 street celebrations in the town.

Disabled Tommy Clingo, chairman of Lynn St Raphael Club and the local Spastics' Society, prepares to start his new car by turning on the ignition… with his teeth. The special adaptations on the car enabled Tommy to drive it without using his hands. The *EDP* spotlighted his courage and determination on 26 March 1973.

Thass a larf!… A jovial pause in the civic pomp during the awarding of the Freedom of the Borough to Alderman Mrs Alice Fisher (at microphone) in October 1962. Among those sharing the joke are, from left, deputy mayoress Eileen Dye, deputy mayor Ted Benefer, mayor Fred Jackson and town clerk Mr E.W.Gocher.

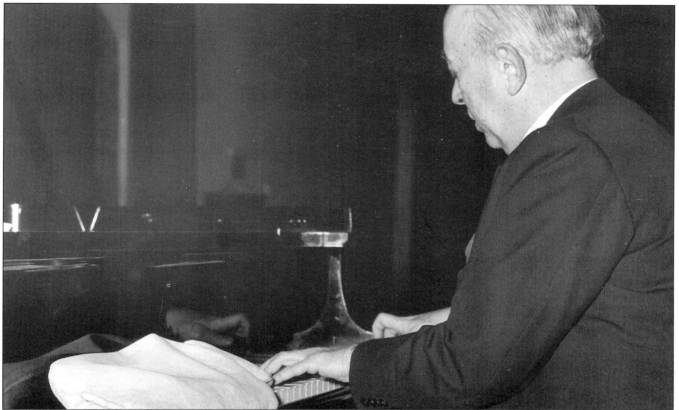

When famous concert pianist Smerterlin came to Lynn for the 100th lunchtime recital at the Guildhall of St George on 12 December 1958 there was just one problem – the keys were too cold. The solution? A hot water bottle, of course. Here Smerterlin warms up…while his keys do the same!

The Bishops of Ely, Lynn and Norwich found themselves in a decidedly unclerical setting in June 1973 – a diocesan tug of war contest. The event was held as part of a tour by the Bishop of Ely, the Rt Revd Dr E.J.K.Roberts. Where the boundary of his diocese met that of Norwich – at West Lynn – Bishop Roberts joined Lynn Bishop the Rt Revd Aubrey Aitken and the Bishop of Norwich, the Rt Revd Maurice Woods, in the tongue-in-cheek battle. Terrington St Clement Junior School tugged for Ely, and West Lynn School (in Norwich City FC kit) kept the Norfolk diocese flag flying.

Lynn police had an unusual runaway on their hands in April 1971 – Georgie the budgie. Georgie, seen here with typist Sally Edeley and police cadet John Robinson, had escaped from the Columbia Way home of Mrs Horsley when her daughter was cleaning his cage. The bird was identified when he spoke his party piece… 'Pretty boy Georgie, give us a kiss'.

King's Lynn Hospital – and hospital radio – volunteers joined forces to help a sponsored bed push through Lynn town centre in September 1978 to raise money for the Handicapped Children's Pilgrimage Trust.

Where did you get that hat? Easter bonnet prize winners Mrs Annie Herriven (83) and Mrs Grace Haverson (75) at the Windsor Park Grouped Homes on 14 April 1973.

It was a fact-finding mission which led a group of Lynn borough councillors to the Walks in March 1973. They were inspecting a track put down by the Lynn and District Society of Model Engineers. Members of the group were seeking backing for a permanent layout. Ex-engine driver Harry Mallett and fellow club member R.Allen provided steam-powered rides for the councillors – and some lucky children.

Joe Parker, one of the last of the generations of travelling tradesmen who were once such an essential part of Norfolk life. Joe, 73, from Clenchwarton, was pictured at North Wootton on 12 June 1973 sharpening scissors and knives – just as his father had done before him.

Fashion at your fingertips… 16-year-old Jennifer Piper from Gaywood models the latest 1965 craze for the *EDP* lens – Pop Art fingernails.

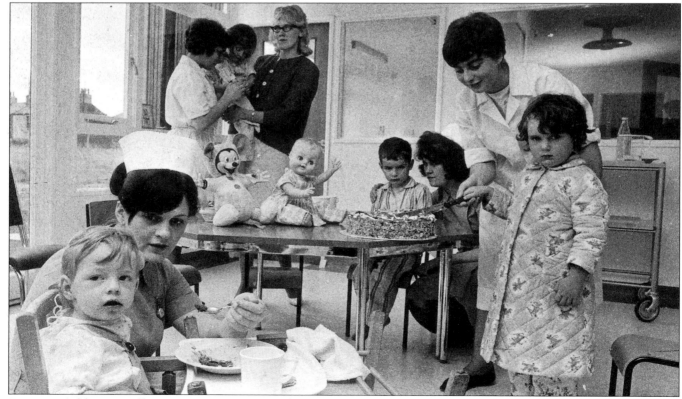

Four-year-old Lyn Collins was 'mum' to cut the cake to open the new £40,000 children's unit at King's Lynn Hospital in July 1966. The unit had two wards, eight single beds and space for 20 children.

Borough mayor Fred Juniper threw himself into his civic role with plenty of energy in his 1975-76 year of office... and ended up in the boxing ring. North Lynn's Fred took on his Peterborough counterpart (and great friend) Bill Cashmore in a bout in a Friars' tournament at the Regis Rooms. After three eventful 90-second rounds, civic pride was shared with a mutual 'knockout'. The fight was staged as part of series of charity events by Mr Juniper, which included parachute jumping, driving a steam engine and going down a coal mine.

Gaywood's Forget-Me-Not Club pictured opening its doors for the first time on 3 March 1966. Aiming to bring together the lonely and the elderly, the club was a ground-breaking joint venture between Anglican, Methodist and Roman Catholic clergy. The *EDP* reported the opening thus: 'For three hours... the members have their lunch and then a gossip – which the ladies said they enjoyed very much – or a game of cards for the men.'

Going for a run in the Walks took on a new meaning for Colin Barrett, of South Everard Street, in January 1976. The *EDP* pictured him with Shiralee, his three-month-old orphaned foal. "It's just like taking a dog for a walk," he said.

Once the opening Mart formalities are over, the civic dignitaries tour the funfair and concentrate on letting their hair down – although when you have a hat that can prove harder than it looks, as Lynn mayor Betty Barton demonstrates. Sharing the fun of the 1977 fair with her were West Norfolk District Council chairman Sir John Bagge and Lady Bagge.

Christmas Time

Christmas is a time for families, carols, presents... and nostalgia. This chapter features a selection of pictures illustrating a wide range of seasonal activities.

One day my prince will come... and he did, to the Howard School's Christmas panto on 14 December 1972 – much to the obvious annoyance of the 'wicked witch'!

King's Lynn Round Tablers in full song at the Fairstead estate in the late 1960s

A row of Christmas trees lends a seasonal air to New Conduit Street in December 1971.

What a present! A visitor to North Lynn Over 60s Club's Christmas Party on 8 December 1971 is clearly delighted with his gift. Lynn High School provided the evening's entertainment, following a tea enjoyed by 130 people from North Lynn and North End. Guest of honour was town mayor Nadai Lumb.

Behind you… Christmas panto and party time at All Saints' School in December 1965.

Carols under the Christmas tree – with the help of members of Lynn Town Band – outside the Duke's Head Hotel, Tuesday Market Place, in the late 1960s.

The 'Minors of ABC' taking part in a post-Christmas fancy dress party at the Majestic Cinema in 1968.

Father Christmas is Here! proclaims the front window poster at Jermyn's store, suitably trimmed up for the festivities in December 1961.

Zap! Ke-pow! and little Alan Hemmings is the envy of his friends in November 1966 as he models Lynn's Number 1 Christmas boys' toy... a Batman outfit. Also high on the wanted list at this Lynn toy store that year were James Bond gizmos and gadgets from *The Man from UNCLE* television series.

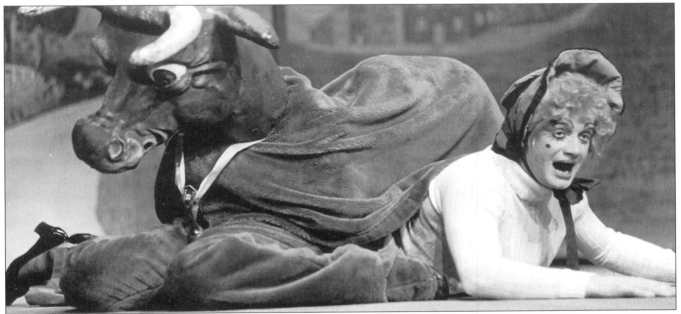

Where would Christmas be without a pantomime? King's Lynn Operatic and Dramatic Society put on *Jack and the Beanstalk* for their Christmas 1972 production and, as Dame Durden (John Blair) discovered, being on stage can present weighty problems. Elizabeth Young played Jack in the Guildhall show, which was produced by Michael Rowlands and Walter Rye.

Come to think of it, where would Christmas be without Santa, either? Father Christmas makes his annual arrival to the obvious delight of children at the 1973 Campbell's Soups Christmas party.

Tales From The River

It is not overstating the case to say the Great Ouse is the reason for Lynn's existence. The source of early riches – and the source of heartache through frequent flooding over the centuries. And, in this chapter, the source of nostalgia as we focus on generations of waterside and waterborne activities.

September 1963, and the buoys on Lynn waterfront proved an irresistible playground for this trio. For, as the *EDP* headline writer put it: 'Buoys will be buoys...'

Almost close your eyes, and with a bit of imagination you could be back in the days of sail... the *Will Everard* was a regular arrival at Lynn port. Here she is on a visit in June 1960.

The traditional service of blessing the nets was revived in May 1978 when the Revd Geoffrey Lang led a service at – where else – the Fisher Fleet.

There's one 'ship' which is permanently moored on the South Quay – the TS *Vancouver*, home of the Lynn Sea Cadets. The *EDP* was on hand in March 1965 to record the visit of Commander J.H.Groom, as part of the Admiralty's annual inspection.

The *Agnes C II* on her way to her launch at Lynn docks in August 1974. She is accompanied by family and friends of the boat's owner, and builder, Frank Castleton. The original *Agnes C* was built by the famous Worfolk brothers.

Getting mighty crowded: 30 August 1967 and while the East German grain ship *Stubnitz* prepares to berth by the Purfleet silos, a timber-laden Russian vessel heads for the docks.

Dramatically foreshortened by the long lens used by the *EDP* photographer, this unusual June 1974 view of the Fisher Fleet contrasts it with the modern main block of the Norfolk College of Arts and Technology in the background. Among the boats berthed in the fleet is the LN219, the *Three Anns*.

The timeless man-made beauty of the Custom House, Lynn's best-loved building, is complemented by the natural delights of the flock of swans bobbing about on the Purfleet high tide. This picture dates from 1975.

The year's most unusual ferry passengers from West Lynn are Christian students who carry a wooden cross as part of their pilgrimage to Walsingham. This was the group making its arrival on the ferry steps on 6 April 1977.

The year? Well, it just had to be the winter of 1962-63... and the dredger BTC *Breckland* lies surrounded by ice in the Alexandra Dock.

You can cross by ferry or by road – but 18-year-old Gary Page decided he'd try another way in October 1971 – flying. Gary, dubbed the 'Bird Man of Lynn', tried his flight as part of the Tech's rag week. Egged on by his friends, the student launched himself off the South Quay… and landed straight in the river. Unbowed, a dripping Gary vowed afterwards he would have another go the following year.

The winter of 1978-79 produced a sight not seen since that 1962-63 winter – ice floes in the Ouse. West Lynn ferryman Reg Hare negotiates the ice on 5 January 1979.

Under billowing clouds, an evocative view of Lynn waterfront taken from West Lynn around 1960.

Familiar Faces

To finish our selection, here is a chapter drawing on the many personalities – both nationally famous and purely local characters – who have visited or lived in Lynn over the years.

Percy Panks finally called it a day from Lynn Cattle Market in November 1975, after working there since – 1903. Percy, 85, seen here with the gold watch he received for 50 years' service, helped look after the livestock at the market. But for generations of Gaywood children, it was Percy's little grocery and sweet shop in Rosebery Avenue – which he opened in 1933 – which they remember with affection.

Comedian Arthur Haynes found an unusual calling in April 1962 – bingo calling, that is. Arthur was at Lynn as celebrity caller for the new Alpha bingo club which opened in the former Theatre Royal cinema in St James' Street. On this opening night, attended by a sell-out 1,000 crowd, queues stretched back along Tower Place.

The 1970 General Election was predicted to be a neck-and-neck affair, and Prime Minister Harold Wilson paid a whistle-stop visit to Lynn on 1 June to boost the campaign of sitting MP Derek Page. He warned party workers not to be complacent about Page's good constituency record being enough to secure re-election. "Don't take any chances," he said. He was right – at the 19 June count, young Tory Christopher Brocklebank-Fowler (seen bottom left at the declaration) edged home after a recount by just 33 votes.

Sooty made his Lynn debut at the ripe old age of 21 on 13 April 1970, with the help of Harry Corbett, naturally. The pair are pictured with two of their entranced audience Gina Oxbrow, six, and Michael Faulkner, five.

His name was Bond, James Bond... George Lazenby, who played 007 in *On Her Majesty's Secret Service*, was at Lynn in 1970 as the guest of the Susan Saint Boutique. The models included Janet Roberts, Liz Ward, Karen McKenna, Valerie Loades and Margaret Balding (née Salmon).

Raymond 'Boz' Burrell was probably the most successful product of the 'Ousebeat' music scene which sprang up in West Norfolk in the early 1960s. Boz, seen here against a Mart backdrop in 1966, was a member of the Tea-Time Four before heading for London and eventually finding fame with King Crimson and Bad Company.

Actress Margaret Rutherford is a study in concentration as she rehearses for a Lynn Festival event in an early 1960s visit.

Brenda Giles' remarkable story began in 1976 when the Gaywood housewife reared five abandoned seal pups in her garden. Dozens of rescued seals – and years of round-the-clock dedication – later, her caring work had brought her national respect, and her work was spotlighted in a television documentary. Mrs Giles was awarded the BEM for her efforts.

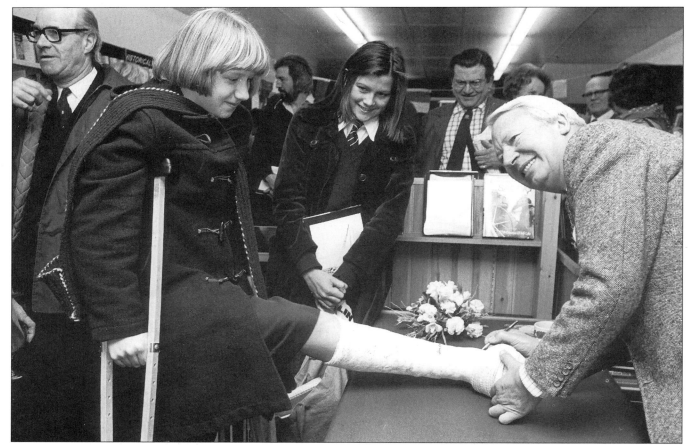

Former Prime Minister Edward Heath must have signed many documents in his time – but chances are he'd never signed a leg before! Lynn High School pupil Henrietta Bruce (14) seized the chance to get Mr Heath's autograph when he visited John Prime Bookshop in Lynn on 26 March 1976. Mr Heath was signing copies of his book *Sailing – A Course of My Life*.

Shirley Williams' place in political history as one of the SDP 'Gang of Four' was still many years away when she was guest of honour at the annual dinner of the women's section of the Lynn Labour party in February 1967. Mrs Williams, then a junior minister in the Department of Education and Science – is pictured with secretary Eve Aveyard (wife of Labour agent Frank), MP's wife Audrey Page (president) and Mrs May Baker (chairman).

Bakery roundsman Ernie Breeze had spent more than half a century making sure the people of Lynn had their breakfast toast on time when he finally called it a day on 27 May 1966. Ernie, of Riverside, Gaywood – seen here delivering in South Lynn – started his career with the Co-op before World War One pushing a handcart, then progressed to a pony and cart and finally an electric van.

A smacker for Lynn bride Mary White from two famous faces... Tony Blackburn and Terry Wogan. Mary (née Titmuss) had worked for showbiz agent Harold Davidson when she wed John White at St Margaret's on 25 August 1973. Other stars on the guest list included pop musician Dave Clark.

A figure inextricably linked with the Lynn Festival, conductor Sir John Barbirolli became a familiar figure round town with his trademark black Verdi hat and cane. Sir John was responsible for bringing the famous Halle Orchestra to the festival on many occasions and was awarded the Freedom of the Borough in 1969. Sadly Sir John collapsed at a festival rehearsal the following year and died a few days later, aged 70.

Top of the Pops dancers Pan's People paid a visit to Lynn on 9 June 1972 to help launch the town's Intercon nightspot. The dancers – Ruth, Louise, Dee Dee, Babs and Andrea – are seen here with club manager Steven Gaunt. For the launch evening, Radio One DJ Alan 'Fluff' Freeman spun the discs.

Lynn's Sheik Michael (alias Michael Taylor) found breaking a world record was hot work on 19 February 1973. He managed to ignite a paraffin-soaked bundle of straw at a distance of eight feet, more than a foot better than the previous record. But he declined to demonstrate one of his other tricks for the camera – sword swallowing. "The taste of the metal gives me tonsillitis," he explained.

What a carry-on... comedy actor Charles Hawtrey was in town on 24 June 1965 to present a prize to Margaret Raby, on behalf of her mother Ivy. The prize was a bridal gown, bridesmaids' dresses and a honeymoon in Malta. Also pictured are Margaret's fiance David Page, cinema manager Charles Horrex and deputy mayor and mayoress Mr and Mrs E.A.Gibbons.

Chief Superintendent Fred Calvert found himself the centre of attention in January 1975 when his long and distinguished career came to an end. Chief Supt Calvert arrived in Lynn in 1945 as the last Chief Constable of the old Borough Police Force, and his 44 years in the force saw him awarded the MBE and the Queen's Police Medal. Out of uniform, Fred was best known throughout West Norfolk and Fenland for his love of the amateur stage, such as this splendid March 1961 picture of him playing Hajj the Poet in a production of Kismet.

It was only six years after *that* hat-trick, so when World Cup star Geoff Hurst arrived at Lynn on 1 September 1972, to promote a range of sportswear, he was assured of an enthusiastic crowd. And that's just what he got.

Subscribers

Mrs J O Abbot

A W Addison

M T Alger

Michael Allfrey

Valerie Kathleen Allison

Maggie Anderson

Anthony Avis

Bruce Barnard

Audrey Ellen Barry (née Hillard)

Mrs L Bateson

A B Bloomfield

T Bly

Mrs V Buckenham

Mrs M K Bullock

Denis A Burton

Mr & Mrs F A Carter

Geof. Carter

Mr P J & Mrs M E Cheatle

Brian Cobbold

S Crane

Mr H C Crome

Michael John Dennis

Mr G Ebbs

Wendy Eke

Ivor A English

Mrs K M Findlay

R C Fiske

Mrs F Fitheridge

W G Gemmell

John Giles

Mrs S M Green

Mr & Mrs Albert Hall

Mr D Harwood

Eileen V Haynes

Eric A Hayter

J Howling

G Huckle

Rosemary Huggins

Mrs D Jackson

Peter Jacobs

Ruth & Ron Jarvis

Krystyna Jenkinson

Peter Jermany

Richard Jermy

E P Jermyn

Mr & Mrs K R Jermyn

Mrs K M Johnson

Barbara & Maurice Kiddle

J M & C P King

Mrs G I Krill

Mark Andrew Larter

Alan T A Lemmon

Mrs Olive E Lemmon

Gordon McCalmont

Mr J M G Mann

K M Mann

George Marshall

Joyce Mason

R W Mason

Mrs S Navarro, Terneuzen, Holland

Mr K H G Nobbs

Richard Parr

Amy & Edgar Pearson

Adam Lindsley Penny

Mrs L A Piggott

R Pritt

P & A Rose

Wendy Rose

David & Tina Rice

Donald C Scott

Janice Simons

Les & Peggy Spinks

Mrs D Statham

Mrs Rose Stevens

Karen J Stewart

Mrs Fiona Taylor

Joy Taylor

Mr M Taylor

Barbara H Thomas

Mr J W Thrower

Grace Tuck

Catherine R E Walker

F Leonard Warner

June Edwina Wasey

S & P Wells

Christopher C Wilkinson

Mr Stephen R Williams

D M Woodhouse